The Path to Success: Famous Secrets
By Dan Van Casteele
Copyright © Dan Van Casteele, 2011 (1st Ed.)
All Rights Reserved.
Copyright © Dan Van Casteele, 2014 (2nd Ed.)
All Rights Reserved.
Copyright © Dan Van Casteele, 2015 (3rd Ed.)
All Rights Reserved.

Table of Contents

INTRODUCTION 7
BACKGROUND 9
HOW I APPEARED ON MTV 11
CREATING A NEW TREND 14
WITHIN THE UNKNOWN 16
THE PATH TO SUCCESS.....................................18
THE FIRST PERFORMANCES 20
ORGANIZING EVENTS 22
BECOMING A FAMOUS DJ 24
THE POWER OF MUSIC 26
MUSIC AS A THERAPY 28
MUSICALITY AND CRITICAL THINKING......30
YOUR PERSONAL VALUE 32
FINDING GOLD IN THE TRASH 33
MAXIMIZING YOUR RESEARCH 35
THE PRICE OF BEING UNIQUE........................36
A SYSTEM WITHIN ANOTHER SYSTEM........38
UPLIFTING WITH MUSIC 40
THE GOOD AND THE BAD...............................42
JUDGMENTS AND REPUTATION 44
THE EFFECT OF BAD DECISIONS 46
BEYOND SOCIAL STEREOTYPES 48
ORIGINALITY..51
TAKING ACTIONS 53
YOUR PUBLIC IMAGE..54
YOUR ARTISTIC NAME 56
THE WRONG ARTISTIC NAME 58
HIDING YOUR IDENTITY.................................60
ONLINE MARKETING..62
BEING DIFFERENT 64

ENTERTAINING AND PERFORMING 65
ATTRACTING FOLLOWERS 67
MANAGING FAME 70
PEOPLE THAT SHOULDN'T PERFORM 72
BEING ATTACKED..74
PRODUCTION AND PERFORMANCE...............77
MIXING WITH A COMPUTER 79
PREPARING SETS FOR PARTIES 80
PRINCIPLES TO CREATE A GOOD SET...........83
COMMITTING TO YOUR VALUES 85
THE IMPORTANCE OF HOMEWORK 87
RECOGNIZING FRIENDSHIPS..........................89
BEING DIFFERENT FROM THE REST 90
CHOOSING A CLUB...94
APPLYING AS A DJ 96
NEGOTIATING YOUR PRICE 98
PROMOTING YOURSELF 100
MAKING FRIENDS 102
BEING IN DANGER 104
HIRING SECURITY GUARDS.........................106
REPLYING TO INVITATIONS 108
THE WORSE THING DJS DO 110
KEEPING YOUR FANS.....................................111
PREPARING FOR A PERFORMANCE 113
DEALING WITH INCOMPATIBILITY 115
DJING STYLES 117
THE ORGANIC DJ 119
EQUALIZING RHYTHMS.................................121
EVALUATING YOUR WORK 123
THE SPIRITUAL ART IN DJING 125
CONTROLLING A PERFORMANCE 126

STRATEGIES ON STAGE...................................129
SIMPLE WAYS TO MIX 130
WORKING WITH OTHERS 132
HAVING FUN 133
INVITING OTHER DJS.......................................134
EVALUATING A DJ...135
REASONS TO ORGANIZE LINE-UPS..............136
SHARING YOUR MEMORIES 138
MANAGING SUCCESS 140
DREAMING WITH A FUTURE..........................142

INTRODUCTION

There are techniques to DJ and to become a music producer. There are also methods to organize music events and to promote them. But, few people ever wrote about what truly makes everything awesome, or which criteria an artist should follow to gain success and reach the level of the most famous.

Even though many would refer to such knowledge as being impossible to gain or organize in obvious principles, this book is based on the biography of a famous DJ, Dan Van Casteele, who has been implementing it all his life to make himself and others successful, and reach top word charts dozens of times.

This book talks about experiences in DJing, organizing parties, managing DJs, producing and composing Music, as well as in competing against the best musicians in the world. And, while not referring to mainstream beliefs, it does show how to be the best in these situations. This is, very likely, one of the most complete manuals about how to be successful in the field of electronic music.

The content of this book may shock you, due to its simplicity and direct approach to complex topics related to the music industry. Nevertheless, the quality of the best DJs is measured by their results, and it's the intention of this book to maximize them, by promoting the use of good strategies and creative approaches to music.

A Musician is, above all things, an Artist and a Dreamer, and this is the book that shows how to combine these three characteristics altogether and efficiently. Anyone has the right to become a DJ, but only those that can use their heart to perform with love for music and are able to uplift the heart of others, should have such opportunity, and it's for them that this book is intended. Here, you'll find the most hidden secrets of the music industry and, if you follow them, your chances of reaching popularity will dramatically increase. It includes descriptions, advices and recommendations about the most vital aspects related to the music career of a DJ.

For 4 years, from 2011 to 2014, this book was classified as a Bestseller on Amazon. So, read it, because nobody will ever tell you about the best kept secrets here exposed!

This book is dedicated to Louise Van de Casteele. May her soul rest in peace! But I would also like to express my gratitude to all the DJs, Producers and Nightclub Managers who collaborated in my projects and made the content here exposed possible.

BACKGROUND

According to many experts, my path to success was extremely quick and unnatural, for someone without any background in music and little knowledge about it. Nevertheless, it wouldn't be possible without so much hard word, dedication, constant studying and analysis of the new tendencies in music, as well as a tremendous effort to achieve uniqueness and maintain a never-ending flow of creativity within me.

My biography isn't similar to many others. I didn't grow up in a family of musicians and my parents weren't educated in music. I have never learned to play a musical instrument, expect flute in school, and I always had bad grades in my examinations, apart from, very honestly, hating these classes. I couldn't do much more than listening to what my friends were enjoying, and trying to understand why, while watching MTV and the German Music Channel VIVA.

As a teenager, I started listening to Bryan Adams and Bon Jovi, and I really liked it. But, I was also a fan of intro music for cartoon series. However, when I started hanging out with fans of Iron Mayden, Metallica and Megadeth, a new world opened for me. I was actually addicted to metal, until I had a first glimpse of techno music from the Channel VIVA. I will never forget the moment I was at home zapping channels and suddenly stumbled upon a live broadcast of the famous Love Parade in Berlin. Carl Cox was playing and that first impression would change me forever. I never really understood what was music, but I knew what felt good, and what Carl Cox was doing was much more than techno or music, it was a new feeling I never had when listening to other musicians. I was 18 years old, and immediately obsessed with electronic music, especially German techno and trance. I couldn't stop thinking about the fact that I had surely been born in the wrong country, as I simply adored all the music coming from Germany. I would be obsessed for the next days, watching the German Charts for Dance music and recording them in my VHS video recorder. I will be listening obsessively and compulsively for the following weeks.

HOW I APPEARED ON MTV

Everything changed in my life, when one day I saw a commercial about eJay music software. I was astonished when realizing that it was possible to create techno and dance music with a computer. So, I spent the following weeks trying to find it. I just wanted to create my own electronic music and had fun with it. It's much different from learning how to play a musical instrument, something I was never good at. The person that got me the software, Dance eJay 2 is today a rich CEO of a multinational company in the field of copper. It's interesting how life unfolds.

I was so thrilled with the idea of creating my own music, that I immediately created a track in that same day, without any knowledge about how to do it, and simply by mixing some sounds and voice samples that I found interesting.

In the following week he got me Rave eJay, and that just made me even more excited with the whole experience. I basically stopped studying for my exams, because I was addicted to creating music.

Soon after that, I saw another commercial, named, "eJay of the Week on MTV" and that moment would change me forever.

In only one year, I learned to appreciate electronic music for the first time, created my first songs with a very basic software, named eJay, and was entering a competition for MTV. I was just having fun, but everything changed when my first track ever, entered the top 15 Europe, and the same happened to my second, third and fourth tracks. I was nominated in a total of 16 times, with different songs. And, that put the whole fun in a new ground. I was now competing to win, against millions of Europeans with background in music, DJs, professional composers and other amazingly talented people with machines plugged to their computers that I couldn't possibly afford to buy, professional singers teaming with them, and the best software they could find. Actually, most producers were using the best software in the world, because this competition didn't had any special requirement, and the uploaded songs were just mp3s.

The difficulties and the logical impossibility to ever reach number one were obvious, but my passion for music never fadeaway, so I persisted, by working harder than ever. Every single night, I would create an average of 2 to 4 songs, and in one year, I published more than 600 songs. As Danny Tenaglia said, "I wake up and eat music for breakfast".

To leverage my opportunities, of being among the top 15 Europe, which was getting harder as time went by, I analyzed the best songs, compared their similarities and differences, and, as I couldn't get better software or have enough money to by hardware to help me, I though about other strategies to win, and they included a very extensive and difficult quest for samples that I could use to create better music with a software that was far too behind my competitors, which now included millions of professional musicians.

In the end, I lost hope, but not persistence. I created new tracks until the last day of the competition, and just when I least expected it, I was the winner, the last winner of the competition, with a song entitled "Goddess of Groove", a new music style, which would later inspire a new trend, seen more prominently with Kylie Minogue "Can't get you out of my head" and Lady Gaga "Bad Romance".

CREATING A NEW TREND

Surely, the best learn with the best, and just like I had learned from the best to reach my place on MTV, namely, Kai Tracid, Cosmic Gate, Westbam, Moguai, Paul Van Dyk, Paul Oakenfold, Carl Cox, Scooter, Alice Deejay and Tiesto, others in the pop music industry did the same, by noticing the fresh ideas of people like me. That's how the music industry works.

The strategy I followed was based in the combination of two styles that I was a fan of, the Dutch and German trance music style, combined with the new wave electronic tracks from the 80s. To this combination, I added a smooth and attractive female vocal, that led many to believe I was using Madonna's vocals. And a great idea for a new tendency in music was born.

Actually, Madonna didn't stay behind in this new genre, as she suddenly reappeared in the music scene in 2005 with a new look, resembling this style I introduced to the world, even though her team of producers definitely took it to a new level, by doing further research on music from the 80s and taking more inspiration from there. The best example is "hung up", even though she was already catching up with "what it feels like for a girl", remixed by the British Above and Beyond, which also inspired me.

I must say that Madonna is probably one of the best examples regarding artists that aren't afraid to reinvent themselves and adjust to new trends, while others fall behind due to lack of insight about the real meaning of doing music. But, within this path, the Black Eye Peas took it to the highest level possible, with titles like "the time". So, now, new artists have to reinvent themselves in order to pursue a new place among the pioneers. I would say that, at this point, it's exhausting to reinvent more 80s styles, but a new trend in classical sounds and opera music could create another flow of creativity into an explored spectrum of sounds. Music is like an ocean of vibrations, in which everyone is simply trying to catch and surf the best waves, but there are always new coming.

WITHIN THE UNKNOWN

I believe that if I hadn't created what I did, somebody else would probably do it. So, it's never as much about being unique, as it is about catching a new trend in the right moment. 10 years later, after being on MTV, this was my most significant lesson, which would then help me become successful in many other areas of my life.

I never got any recognition for that, and hard it is to prove what I just said. However, I don't feel the need to show evidences of these statements, just like I didn't feel the need to justify my faith in my work before, when I was completely alone, believing in my success, in a very difficult moment of my life, when my parents where divorcing and I had to restart college in a new university, while having all my friends and colleagues believing I had lost my mind for expecting to be on MTV music television. I wasn't studying well, because all I had on my mind were strategies to download new music samples, so nobody wanted to work with me and I had to do every college assignment by myself. I was also not eating well, because I wanted to save enough money to buy CDs with professional samples, and I wasn't sleeping well, because I would produce music from 11pm to 6 am, and then sleep for 3 hours before going to college. I was also practicing two martial arts at the same time, so the pressure I had put on my shoulders was huge.

That victory on MTV, in August 2001, felt really good, after so much hard work and criticism from others. I was laughed at, until my face was in front of everyone, on their TV screens, in November 2001, as the best music composer in Europe. This achievement changed my personality forever, but it was just the beginning of my journey in music.

THE PATH TO SUCCESS

After being awarded best music producer on MTV in 2001 and have a videoclip broadcast by MTV International, I received the attention of many artists that sent emails congratulating me for this achievement. And, because I really loved music, I invited them to do music with me. From this gathering of artists, a group was created. We named it first LouVdC & Co & Friends and later on as MAO (Musique Assistée par Ordinateur).

Louise Van de Casteele was one of the music producers competing with me for MTV, while living in Belgium and in her 60s. She gladly created this group and managed it afterwords. Thanks to her, we've all created projects together, which involved exchanging ideas, samples, software, etc. I really learned a lot from this group, composed of people from all over the world, namely, France, Belgium, Germany, Russia, England and the USA, among other countries. Thanks to them, my achievements never ended.

In the second competition for eJay, in 2002 and following the previous, one my songs, remixed by Louise, reached NR.2 world. In 2003, I was nominated NR.1, best world producer, in two different charts, dance music and techno, by vitaminic.com. In that same year, was also the NR.8 musician in the UK Charts at Besonic.com. And, following that, I got over

30 tracks among the top 20 world for trance music on Besonic as well.

During this time, I started publishing my first albums in France and Belgium, due to several requests from fans in these countries and with the help of Louise.

In July 2009 I wasn't producing new music anymore, but noticed, by accident, that I was top30 in the Belgium Charts for professional musicians at Myspace.com, following Kate Ryan as NR.1. So, as I don't check it regularly anymore, I guess my old tracks may still be somewhere positioning themselves among the best in the world. I now that in 2014 and 2015, for example, many of those tracks created in 2006, were reaching positions such as Nr.1 on soundlick.com, and many others climbed to top10 lists rather quickly.

From what I know as well, my music has been played on Galaxy Net Radio, eJay Radio, Besonic Radio, Radio Channel Z and Red Line, as well as severalClubs throughout Europe and the USA.

THE FIRST PERFORMANCES

As my recognition grew, and my music started being played by other DJs, invitations to perform as a DJ started to spontaneously arrive, coming from different countries, namely, Belgium, Netherlands, Germany, Portugal and USA.

The first performances occurred in college parties and success was immediate, sometimes causing an early end of secondary dance floors, due to the fact that everyone was in my area dancing. To be more precise, 3000 people in a small dance floor, just in the first event. But I was mostly surprised when this happened with very famous DJs that were playing in the main dance floor, near the entrance, DJs that I wasn't really competing with, because I didn't though I had a chance.

From 2003 to 2006, I decided to experience the most diverse environments and audiences, as a way to know more closely different styles, sounds and genres, beyond the music itself, and also as a way to challenge myself. Among different genres I performed with, are Eurotrance, House, Tribal, Electro, Pop, HipHop, Arab, Chillout, Metal, Gothic, Darkwave, Industrial, Hardocore-Techno and Hardstyle, among many others.

Success was always achieved in all these situations and people loved the performances.

In just two years, my fan pages had, all together, over ten thousand subscribers. So, I decided to take things to a new level and this included organizing my first events.

ORGANIZING EVENTS

I started a partnership with several companies in which I had worked before to form my own and clubs where I had performed regularly. The help of many DJs, magazine writers and music shops' owners, helped me with the rest, and the launching was explosive from the beginning.

During this period, I also promoted, taught how to DJ and Produce music, and introduced to the music industry dozens of new talents, most of them in the field of alternative music, which was something I was more willing to explore and promote, in order to show new ideas and creative talents to the world. These events were very popular, which allowed these DJs to become famous suddenly and out of nowhere. Many of them, without any previous experience.

Some of these musicians would later gain more recognition and become well-known in the music industry with several videos on television, namely, in France. But, the same happened to those clubs, which started appearing in the TV news, after catching the attention of several reporters.

During this time, I organized the first Hardocore-Techno events ever made in Portugal in 2006, which had different names, culminating with Gabber Planet in 2007. It was an attempt to create a Portuguese Thunderdome or Qlimax and, for one person alone, in a small country like Portugal, without any financial sponsorship, it was really something big, influencing millions of followers, in some cases, coming from abroad, namely, Italy, Netherlands, Germany, and even South America.

This was possible due to an immense network of friends in the music industry that helped me with the advertisement and promotion. Most of the first clubbers in these events were actually followers of other styles, more alternative in the Portuguese music scene, such as Techno, Psytrance, Industrial and Gothic.

As many professionals recognized, these events were interesting, well-organized and with a very good selection of original new talents, reasons why they were so popular, at least, until I decided to abandon the whole project to become a writer, and later emigrate to Asia, this time to explore new cultures and lifestyles. Among other countries, I've lived the most in China, Singapore, The Philippines, Thailand, Malaysia, Indonesia and India. But, once a DJ, always a DJ, so after being invited so many times, I ended up performing in Asia as well, and realizing that I'm still loved in the music scene after so many years have passed.

BECOMING A FAMOUS DJ

I became quickly famous for being the best and most popular Hardstyle/Hardcore Rave DJ in Portugal, and my name, when invited to other events, was always placed on top of the line-up to attract more people. This happened due to the immense investment I did in promoting amateur music from around the world and mixing it with classics, such as what today is commonly seen on Qlimax events in the Netherlands. The way I performed in 2006 was very similar to what is today seen in this country. So, maybe Portugal took all these years to finally organize its own Rave Parties, but I made it reach a new level or, at least, the highest I could. In its second edition, we had people coming from different European countries to participate and DJs from all over the world, including Germany and countries as far as Chile, offering themselves to perform for free, merely in return for a place to stay and sleep.

Last, but not least, among many things, I was known for mixing Classical Music, Opera, religious sounds, sounds of animals, political speeches, samples of war movies, samples of horror movies and samples of cartoons, in my performances. The style was particularly known for being unique, new, original and always unexpected. In only 7 years, I really did a lot as a musician, and was even invited to play in the Lisbon Music Parade in 2007, but I'm mostly proud of the experience, which is irreplaceable and unique. I learned a lot, with both the good and the bad, and became more mature in my perspective about music and talent, after recruiting, training and working with so many DJs and Producers, many of them with far more experience than me. I was known by many names, such as Genius DJ (aka. Genius Deejay), Dan Van Casteele, Daniel Oakmar and The Pervertborg, and my music can be found nowadays on Amazon and many other platforms for purchase as well as for free download. I eventually published 15 Albums with about 140 of my best tracks among hundreds of them.

In these latest years, I still occasionally perform as DJ, mostly for fun, because I continue to be invited due to my background, and because I'm often offered huge sums of money to play live again. I've also been receiving full-time job offers to be a residential DJ. Therefore, I've been traveling around the world as a writer and musician.

It's my believe today that anyone has the right to become a DJ, but only those that can use their heart to perform, in their love for music, and are able to uplift the heart of others, should have such opportunity, and it's for them that this book is mostly intended and dedicated. I always believed that there are differences between artists that are musicians and musicians that want to be artists. And, I choose to support the firsts.

THE POWER OF MUSIC

One of the most basic things about becoming a DJ is that you must love music. You must be ambitious enough to say, like Jeff Mills, "I love music more than I love people". This means standing above your life experiences and problems, while getting inspiration from them to express your feelings and thoughts.

Music was never another reality for me, but rather a second home, where I was actually feeling safer and stronger. It was also a special dimension of being, where I was able to rebuild myself. And, this was extremely important during my parents' divorce. But, it also had a very important role when I had difficulties to fit in college or deal with my professors arrogance and rudeness. The strength I got through music, transformed me into someone else and, even though I wasn't interested anymore in being social, I did became the President of the Student's Union, thanks to that new powerful feeling coming from within. I was appreciated, admired and voted, because this same power was recognized by others. This power I'm talking about can assume many names, such as charisma, confidence, enthusiasm or simply vitality, even though it can also be easily misinterpreted as arrogance by others. Nevertheless, it does reinforces your character and your nature. The anger in me was transferred into very aggressive sounds and the scorn I felt into music parodies, such as what we see in Eminem's style.

This, I believe now, by looking back at my achievements, is what made the difference. Great talents in music aren't just doing music; they're expressing themselves and sending a message.

MUSIC AS A THERAPY

Within the skills, born from the need to live in a kind of musical Land and communicate through sound, came, others, related to critical thinking and critical analysis. This happened, because you can't be honest to yourself and indifferent to the world at the same time. It doesn't work this way. The more you analyze your emotions, in order to find a suitable channel and process to express them, the more you develop your critical analysis as well. The skills developed through musical expression are profoundly related to cognitive development and self-awareness.

An Artist is someone that learns how to think about his own thoughts and read his own emotions. After that, he'll be the most critical person of his own work, because he'll be the first to listen it, and he'll also listen more than anyone else.

There's no such thing as doing music without thinking about it, and that's why alcoholics and drug addicts in the music business are far more exceptions that they are common. Society and the media makes us believe otherwise, because people tend to develop the tendency to negatively comment about those they admire as a way to bring them down to their level. It's easier than to uplift themselves higher. Our world isn't necessarily prone to promote and accept creativity, and that's something artists have to live with. Before you reach anywhere in life, you'll be severely criticized, mocked and attacked, by those that are closer to you. Only when you pass this barrier, can you get some recognition, usually, from those that have never met you.

MUSICALITY AND CRITICAL THINKING

It's important to learn to appreciate music, specially the newest and most original. And, in order to do this, you must go to websites where amateur DJs are giving us the shortcut. This includes all those platforms where anyone can upload their mixes. Although, you may want to start by those with the highest ranking in a particular genre, and the ones presenting a list of the tracks used, so you can find them as well.

Another way to do a good research on new tendencies includes, obviously, reading magazines that are already doing the best work for you. And, last but not least, you should go to websites where amateur music producers are uploading their work, created with inspiration and without any expectation related to profiting from it. In this way, you'll know where inspiration is flowing and what kind of ideas seem more interesting. Again, you may want to start by the top of a chart in a particular genre related to your own. But, then listen to as much as 100 tracks or sets from each of those charts. In the end, you'll have a much deeper insight about where the wave of creativity is flowing and, naturally, you'll gradually build your own ideas. When those ideas are clear enough, you'll know what to do regarding both music composing and DJing.

Nobody creates anything new; we're all reinventing ourselves and reinventing music with what is available. There's nothing wrong with it and being both humble and honest about it is the best attitude to climb to the top and be among the best, because they all know this already.

Don't force yourself to enjoy the trash, just because somebody told you that it is good, or because that artist won a certain prize! And, don't believe in everything you listen on TV and radios, or see on updated charts! There's a very aggressive marketing machine controlling all those channels. And, Artists that reach them are often just showing the end of their race, and not really their most unique work. Most of the music I played during my career as a DJ wasn't appreciated enough, until it reached TV and famous radios. Then, people accepted it very well. At that point, DJs weren't afraid to play the same as me anymore.

YOUR PERSONAL VALUE

As a DJ, you can choose the shortcut, and just play what people expect, or you can take risks and play something different, that may damage your reputation. But, that's the whole purpose of DJing. If you're not doing something unique, even when mixing music created by others, you're not doing art.

There's a direct relation between being a DJ or producer and being ourselves. If you're not playing something according to your own vision of the world, you're not making art and you're missing the whole purpose of the experience in being a DJ. In other words, you won't evolve in the field and that's why DJs that only follow a trend, are easily surpassed by any other, independently of how many years of experience they may have.

The reason why I was able to achieve a quicker success than many other DJs I met, with more years' experience, is related to the fact that I was able to take risks that they were too afraid to accept. Nevertheless, that's the whole principle of life. You're either living life or you're dying in it. Those creating a new future never die. They feel eternally young and their work is immortalized by the ones that can recognize its value.

FINDING GOLD IN THE TRASH

In order to find good material and original productions, you must be willing to look in and seek for gold in the trash. This trash is basically composed of all the unknown artists that will never reach anywhere and don't care much about it. They are part-time producers or often just kids having fun with music. But, among all this trash of ideas discarded after serving its emotional purpose, you'll also find gold. And, this gold, is related to highly talented individuals that, more often than not, have no idea or conscience about their own quality, because nobody has ever recognized it before. We call them gold in the trash, because you do have to listen to a lot of trash before finding such gold. My average was 300 songs for each 2 that really surprised me.

I almost always tried to contact these artists to give them a chance to work with me, ask about royalties related to using their music but, to my surprise, the vast majority wasn't even interested in bringing their level to a professional ground or didn't believe that their work was worth it, probably due to other issues related to self-esteem.

I like to think about them as street fighters. There are many individuals out there that could easily beat a professional Kickboxer, but are just not interested in doing sports or competing with their talent. This said, the main point I want to transmit here is that you do have more to learn from these people than from the superstars you worship. At some point in life, every single DJ and music producer was a nobody, unknown and unseen among the trash, and they had to make themselves visible with every opportunity they were able to reach. Only those that were humble enough to learn with everyone, while believing in themselves, climbed above the majority, even their own teachers and mentors.

MAXIMIZING YOUR RESEARCH

It's difficult to do everything by yourself, so if you can have friends helping you, that gives you an upper advantage.

I used to be so curious and eager to get the most original music out there, that I would ask for the help of friends addicted to video games that didn't mind downloading music for me while playing games on their computer.

The purpose of all this experience is to start creating your own path. This is the beginning of your journey as a DJ and Producer.

I've met many talented people without ideas, that couldn't stop creating new and interesting tracks after getting inspired by Amateur talents. It's also probably better to start from here, instead trying to copy The Prodigy or Roger Sanchez.

You must find what kind of sounds and music genres get you more easily addicted! Then, you must follow this path, because music is where you heart is as well! You must listen and play what moves you the most!

THE PRICE OF BEING UNIQUE

Everyone told me that if I wanted to make serious money and develop a career as a DJ, I would have to play House Music. And, it's true that the most famous Portuguese DJs in the world, such as Diego Miranda, Rui da Silva and Pete Tha Zouk are all House DJs, But, I would have never become the Nr.1 DJ in Hardcore/Gabber in Portugal, if I had considered those suggestions.

Surely, playing Hardcore made me spend more time with teenagers than with hot models, made me work harder to promote my events, gave me more problems related to jealousy and seriously mental disturbed individuals, but nothing will ever replace the amazing feeling I had when playing my favorite tracks, including my own productions, with a very loud, fast and powerful sound to millions of clubbers shouting like crazy in front of me.

I was very proud of myself, while if I had chosen to play House I could only be proud of being famous or getting loads of money and babes around me.

Surely, it's all great and good, but there are many other ways to reach these goals.

DJs playing music for these purposes have lost the true meaning of doing music, and went from the top to the trash, even though delusional achievements make them believe otherwise. But, that's the difference between being arrogant about your success and proud of your work.

A SYSTEM WITHIN ANOTHER SYSTEM

Most DJs are proud to be filmed and photographed with beautiful models and earn big payments. But, many prostitutes feel the same kind of pride, when being seen with famous politicians and getting well-paid to have sex with them.

That's the whole problem rotting the music industry. Most musicians have sold themselves already. The music industry makes sure this happens, and money or fame, at a certain point in life, can be crucial.

Famous DJs in their 20s are looking for social recognition and lose it when arriving there, because they can't create in a professional level.

DJs in their 40s and late 30s, are basically trying to pay their bills and quit their lame daily job, serving drinks to boring people, working in coffee shops, working in music shops or cleaning toilets in hotels.

It's sad to notice that our world system doesn't promote creativity and talent, but you're either creating your own system or losing yourself within another.

You have to create your own believe system, your basic requirements, your goals and, above all, your vision for yourself.

There are many ways to become famous, attract good-looking women and be well-paid, but the whole purpose of enjoying music must always be present.

In order to get all these things, however, you have to work very hard. And, most people will never tell you how many years of humiliation and poverty they have suffered before transforming their dreams into a reality, because they don't even want to remember it.

In fact, many suffer the same and reach nowhere in life. And, that's why it's as noble as it is wise, to encourage other musicians, work with them and form a team with mutual respect and cooperation.

UPLIFTING WITH MUSIC

Throughout my life, I was not only proud to be a great DJ, but also to work with DJs from different countries and those that needed my support to climb higher. And, more than my own success, I'm also very proud to have been able to build a team of DJs around me, that were mutual supportive.

Every time one of us was playing, the others will encourage him, either by being next to him to help in any need, or in the dance floor, motivating the audience, and uplifting the whole scene.

In my events, I've never abandoned any of the other DJs, and often disregarded any competitive feelings among us. In fact, I promoted healthy competitions, in which we would try to help each other reach the most uplifting reactions. This included playing VJ, when one in our team of DJs was playing music, or mixing music with them.

It was common to see 2, 3 or even 4 DJs mixing music together in our events. And, at some point, nobody really knew who was the leading DJ anymore. And, it didn't really matter, because we were doing it for the thrill of that moment.

In the end of the night, we would have much stronger friendships than ever. And, this, I have never seen in any other group.

In fact, jealousy and aggressive competition are much more common among DJs. If I'm very good at what I do, I won't be able to easily make friends with other DJs, and that's actually something very normal. They'll tend to do their best to give you the worse moments of the parties, when the dance floor is empty or the crowd is demotivated and bored with their bad music.

That's one of the reasons why it's so important to have a leader in these teams, independently of how many years of experience he has.

THE GOOD AND THE BAD

Often, the DJs I was managing were much older than me and much more experienced, but they trusted my guidance and we all became great friends.

Some of us worked in the music industry and helped promoting the others when they had performances alone. Others, were Sports instructors and started teaching Kickboxing to the rest. And, others worked in shops selling remote-controlled cars, and allowed us some fun moments racing against each other. While others where Buddhists and gave us all a change to learn from them.

Basically, it was all much more than music. It was a very rich life experience, full of fun, supporting attitudes and ideas. And, honestly speaking, like me, you may have to be very assertive to reach these goals. This includes avoiding all those Artists that are trying to take advantage of people with more experience and knowledge, to climb over them.

Unfortunately, some of these DJs, immersed in their own egocentric achievements, started doing this, and such behavior was their lost.

Mutual respect in these groups is very important, so when we have to place the names of the DJs performing, we need to take into consideration who we want to put on top and in which order. Moments like this can be sensitive, but a big part of the success of a DJ consists in cooperating with other people.

Finally, there are also others that got lost in the world of drug addiction, and it's sad to see very talented individuals playing without creativity and believing they're still great, after taking those drugs.

JUDGMENTS AND REPUTATION

Throughout your path as a musician, you need to learn to be wise, before making any decision that can jeopardize both your image as your opportunities.

One of the main things to know is that you can't force yourself to like something you don't, but you shouldn't refuse it just because you can't understand it.

When some of the DJs asked me for permission to bring strippers to our shows, and others asked for changes to bring Drag Queens, I had to seriously think about it.

The same thing happened when I was asked for permission to bring Tecktonic Dancers.

The problem with each one of these decisions, isn't necessarily the appearance of what it seems, but always the implications it will bring.

People are attracted by what they see and want to identify with, so even though, apparently, it seems that these "free" performances will attract more audience and create an astonishing show, it will actually affect the root of the purpose behind it. So, it's much more about knowing if it feeds the initial purpose or not.

Most DJs don't really care about where they play music, as long as they're being paid and getting some attention, but that's not wise. Playing in the right place with the right audience is a smarter investment, even though initially it may seem like a lost bet.

I did had bad luck sometimes, by organizing an even or playing in a day in which another, bigger party, was happening in the surrounding area. But, show must go on, and you still have to perform as if you had thousands of people in front of you. It's a business as well, and the owner of the Club needs your commitment to your performance to survive as best as he can during that night.

So, to answer any question, I have never allowed any of the previous groups of dancers to perform in the same place as me.

Those events weren't big enough to have an unbreakable image, at least, from my point of view. Besides, the whole structure of the event would change and the musical style would be affected. And, I wasn't willing, at that point, to do such thing.

THE EFFECT OF BAD DECISIONS

Whatever I may have done when organizing events, didn't stop other two groups, much greedier than me, from copying what I was doing and bring everyone they could get into their party, including, their own grandmother and the kids from their neighborhood.

Needless to say, that they lost credibility in many Clubs and the trust of their owners, as well as the attention that my events initially brought to the Hardstyle and Gabber scene.

They were able to survive for as long as I was playing in other events, because people don't really have much criteria when choosing a party, but they did finish like a tree without water, once I decided to stop playing live in Portugal.

They may never see the relation between both situations, but I had already predicted it and even posted about it, years before my decision was made.

Today, they still have no clue to why their parties can't have more than 10 of their closest friends, including their girlfriends and relatives, and have to be organized in the basement of a nearly bankrupt nightclub.

They will probably never know why, but the explanation is here.

For those that know how, it's easy to build reputation, even if it takes time, but for those that don't, hard work will never payback for them, and their fame lasts a very short period of time.

Besides, it's not wise to attack someone playing the same music as us, just because we fear competition. It's much wiser to promote both parties and avoid conflicts between people. Especially, when we're talking about someone like me, which made all their events possible, after years in which they could only dream about it.

The best thing in my parties is that I was making so many efforts to promote great DJs, and interesting atmospheres, by inviting many VJs to play, that even when my performance wasn't as good as I would expect, the party was still a huge success, thanks to the whole team.

However, what I noticed in other events copying mine, is that everyone was struggling for recognition, without any team work, and that's how they collapsed.

Arrogance kills the DJ and envy is the worse enemy of an Artist. One is socially toxic and the other corrupts creativity.

BEYOND SOCIAL STEREOTYPES

When analyzing other Djs or music producers, don't think too much about their background, because you would be surprised about how unpredictable talent can be.

It's a fact that some of the best world rappers have Irish background and some of the best world techno DJs have African ancestry.

Especially nowadays, things aren't as linear as before. People have access to the same music and opportunities, and this happened mostly with the advent of Internet, which is still evolving, but has only recently really provided a new leverage for everyone.

In modern times, if you're dedicated enough and read books about how to become successful in music, you can go very far in life and develop your talent to a level you've never expected to achieve.

It's interesting to study the history of music as well, because you can learn a lot from it. For example, you may be curious in knowing that the phenomenon of Dance Mania, or the need to dance randomly, was firstly known as a Dancing Plague, and started in the 7th century, but the biggest outbreak occurred in 1375 in

Germany and involved groups of people dancing erratically, sometimes thousands at a time. It affected men, women, and children, who danced until they collapsed from exhaustion.

It's ironic how the first music festivals were known for being madness but were the precursors of the famous Love Parade in Germany, and many other events, as well as the fact that people would dance until they collapsed without the need for any drug.

Other interesting facts you should read about to expand your mind include:

* Knowing that one of the most popular music genres today, House Music, started with small gay communities;

* Heavy Metal started with those that were willing to bring rock n' roll to a new level, by creating electronic guitars, being criticized when appearing for the first time in public;

* Many of today's' Hardstyle and Hardcore Djs, were simply bored with all the other music genres and wanted to created faster music;

* Some of the friendliest musical events today, actually started as being fascist parties to promote neo-nazism;

* Or that, some musical events, even though armless, always faces a big wave of protesters from Christian Churches.

The world changes rapidly and what is new and amazing today, often comes in the most unpredictable ways, like everything else in life.

What is rejected and attacked today, may be worshiped tomorrow. This is true for both music genres and Artists.

ORIGINALITY

If you follow what others are doing, you'll always be just one more.

You'll never be someone by copying others' tendencies or their techniques. And, even if you attach yourself to someone popular, you'll never be anything more than a shadow of that person.

If you want to be unique and original, the one everyone will be talking about, you must find your own path in music, your own uniqueness and, basically, learn to pay attention to where you feel more madness and energy coming from.

Listen to as much different music and unknown producers and DJs as you can. Then, start your own selection. Delete the music that doesn't inspire you to dream and sets that don't motivate you.

In the end of this process, you'll probably finish with only a few tracks and sets. But, those results make you who you are, so you do need to learn to be selective in your work.

The final selection defines you and will allow you to learn more about yourself and what you want to do in music.

If your musical taste can be too diversified, don't worry about it, as that's also how you find yourself. Moby, Daft Punk, the Chemical Brothers and Fat Boy Slim, are all very good examples of producers that found their way in a completely unique style.

Music isn't so much about the sounds, rhythms, speed, or even genres, but the feelings behind them, the message you want to pass and the perceptions you wish to awake in others.

Focus on what you love without paying too much attention to names, popularity or music genres, and you'll eventually understand the meaning of being original and proud about it!

TAKING ACTIONS

Dreaming isn't enough in an extremely competitive and difficult world. If you want to be among the best, you must be willing to work very hard to get there.

As you awaken your conscience and empower your heart, by listening to your favorite music and mixing it, imagination will let you dream about having millions of people in front of you, enjoying your performance. And, there's nothing wrong about this, except that you must put your feet on the ground and work as hard as your dream demands it.

Your self-esteem is built with dreams, and that's how basically I taught dozens of DJs to perform well. I first introduced them to their potential success. And, once they feel comfortable with that, the rest is much easier.

As Sander Kleinenberg says, "Sometimes you need to shake up your own world and the people around you". But, that's not all, as you must be willing to shake yourself as well, and forget all the limiting thoughts you've ever assumed about yourself.

People will forgive your mistakes. if you have the confidence to do a good job. Never underestimate yourself!

YOUR PUBLIC IMAGE

Your self-image starts with the creation of a logo, because you need a brand that people can recognize, as we have too many DJs in the world, and often not with enough quality to be named that.

Make sure this image is professional enough, as it will represent you and bring forth the first impressions about who you are to others. It should be, somehow, cool, and if it has some girls next to you is even better. DJs are often measured by their sex-appeal, even though I can't really explain why.

Actually, it doesn't really matter if you know the people in the pictures you use to advertise yourself, as nobody will ever ask it. You can simply enter a Club and ask some hot girls to take pictures with you. It's as simple as that.

Personally, I prefer profile pictures that don't reveal your face entirely, giving a certain mystery look and leaving people on the expectation of knowing how you really look like. Foggy and light effects are useful for this purpose, so a picture taken like this will do just fine.

Make sure you bring a friend with you to take as many photos as possible in the first time you perform life, even if only for 10 to 15 minutes.

People will judge you immediately from those images and your name will start building a reputation from there. This is your public portfolio, because we live in an extremely visual society, where nobody has patience to read whatsoever or listen to demo sets.

YOUR ARTISTIC NAME

When choosing an artistic name, make sure that it's simple, unique and easy to memorize. That's the criteria to build a list of followers in your parties.

Your name should also provide a certain impact on others and sound meaningful, while not appearing arrogant to other DJs or offensive to the public.

Due to these reasons, simple and neutral names are usually the most chosen. However, for the purpose of exemplification, I will mention the best and the worse names to choose from, based on the names of TOP World DJs on DJ-Mag.

Good Artistic names are, for example, Hardwell, Tiesto, David Guetta, Nicky Romero, Nervo, Above & Beyond, Daft Punk, Paul Van Dyk, Bobina, Infected Mushroom, Cosmic gate, Bob Sinclar and Umek.

Bad Artistic names are, for example, Avicii, Dimitri Vegas, Steve Aoki, Dash Berlin, Skrillex, Deadmau5, Markus Schulz, Knife Party and Fedde Le Grand.

As I have divided the previous names into two groups, it becomes very easy to notice that the names in the first list are much more familiar than the ones in the second, even though their quality or position in the ranking doesn't necessarily seem to be affected by their name.

The problem with having a name that isn't easily remembered is that people will forget you easily if you don't keep building your reputation. Names like Tiesto, David Guerra and Paul Van Dyk, for example, are among the Top 100 World DJs for many years, but I'm sure the others in the second list won't stay there for too long.

Especially in current times, people's memory is very short, and just like you lose friends easily, you'll lose fans even faster. And, that's why it's important to keep them aware of your name.

When choosing this name, make sure as well that it defines you, so that those that want to know you better don't get disappointed.

THE WRONG ARTISTIC NAME

It's not easy to choose a name that won't create abnormal reactions and that's why famous DJs have opted for neutral names.

A Latino calling himself Dan Van Casteele, will surely have problems, for example. The same applies to names like Genius DJ, which tend to be hated by other DJs.

I had to learn this by doing mistakes, and after so many achievements, it's too late to change it.

If I want to build myself in the music industry again, I have to restart from the beginning, with a completely new image and name.

People will forgive these changes once you become famous, but not before that.

What I just said also applies when you want to create music or sets in different genres. It was a big problem when I decided to change from Trance to Hardcore. People aren't as open-minded as they want others to believe. We live in a world of very dumb humans and this dumbness can turn against you, for doing nothing wrong, such as putting your artistic name attached to different genres.

If you play Psytrance and your fans go see you perform Techno or House, you will have problems and lose a big part of them. So, if you wish to work in different fields, divide yourself in different logos and names.

HIDING YOUR IDENTITY

What you do will also be related to who you are as a DJ. So, make sure nobody will ever know who you are.

In some situations, it can be as humiliating as also shocking and pathetic.

As an example, one of the most famous Psychiatrists in Portugal, enjoys wearing masks of monsters in rave events, while playing music naked and crawling on the floor like a dog, making himself look like the worse performer I've ever seen in public.

Apparently, nobody ever noticed this fact. But, what would you think it I told you that this person is also the President of the Portuguese Association for Schizophrenia?

On the other hand, people tend to associate you with what you do, so even though they may not seem to care about seeing a Psychiatrist making a fool of himself in a rave party, they would feel embarrassed if knowing that their DJ is a member of a political organization or a religious society with many haters.

I've actually lost many fans because of this last issue.

Supposedly, people should live in a religious and political free world, at least in Europe. But, this only applies in theory, as nobody acts according to how they should, and the law is only useful for those that can afford it. Besides, discrimination is not really something people would write about; it's just what they do.

A DJ is somehow like a Superhero. It doesn't matter how good or bad your job is, as you simply can't reveal your daily life identity.

Your music fans can only know you as a musician, and you must make sure they can't find anything about you online. The less people know about you, the more they'll respect you.

Unfortunately, this is how it works. I'm not making the rules, but simply warning you about them, after being severely punished in many blogs for just being myself.

The more famous you become, the more attention you get. The result of it depends on how prepared you were.

ONLINE MARKETING

Once you have an artistic name and logo, it's time to promote yourself online.

Pages like Facebook, Myspace and Twitter, are basic. You should do more, and publish your work online, in music platforms, and in as many as you can find, but also on Youtube.

In fact, you should use Youtube to communicate with your fans and leave more personal videos. Most DJs only post their performances, but fans also want to see you talk, they want to know how you think about music and Djing, so answer these kind of questions and you'll be even more respected as a musician.

To make it more simple and credible, you can invite a friend to interview you,

Make sure you create a webpage as well. It should be simple and provide links to your albums and music.

Offering something for free, like some songs and music samples, or even wallpapers, is also a strategy to attract more people to your websites.

In one of the pages, write your biography, musical preferences and other things that you believe to be interesting for fans to know.

What you love to listen also defines your personality. So, don't focus merely in mentioning famous musicians as your favorite. This makes you look cheap.

Do some research and concentrate your efforts in advertising new talents that nobody ever heard about!

BEING DIFFERENT

If you want to be unique and admired, you must provide reasons that justify it, and they imply educating people to your musical preferences.

To give you an example, while all the European DJs were looking at Europe, especially Holland, for Hardcore and Hardstsyle, I went beyond and focused on talents from South America and Japan.

That's how I overcome my competition by very far away. I was unique, original and using music with quality at the same time.

Some loved my parties and others hated me even more. But, that's the price of talent. You can't expect everyone to like you.

The interesting part in this history is that, every single person that hated me, never missed one of my performances. So, I'm not sure what to think about DJs that spent days dedicating themselves to write hateful words, and spreading negative rumors about me, but then came to my parties and danced from beginning to end in every single one of them.

In the following day, they would post more spiteful words about the experience there, but the fact is they have never missed any of my events.

ENTERTAINING AND PERFORMING

A DJ is a leader, not a follower.

This is very basic, but only a very few DJs I met knew it, and they were always among the most successful.

To be a leader, you must understand the meaning of it.

It basically means that you won't give people what they want, just because they want it. There's a difference between playing music for clubbers, or having a performance where people come specifically to see your act.

I always made sure I was seen as a performer, and that shaped the character of my image as a musician. Nobody ever forgot it.

However, that's why others playing with me were always easily forgot in the following days. They were just entertaining people.

You can choose to be an entertainer, but you should be, foremost, a performer. For me, they represent totally different things.

A DJ that is an entertainer has no idea of what he will do in a nightclub. He will bring hundreds of CDs with him, and hope that people will like his random choice. He will just try to play what people seem to want and make them happy.

But, a DJ that is a performer, has already prepared the whole set in advance, will bring a few albums with him, and will play exactly that. He's going to do a show and is very sure of his results. He can't fail, but he invests everything he has on that particular set.

Often, because they plan their set in advance, they focus more on remixes and special effects, which enhances the dance floor experience to a new level, much more interesting to witness.

In order to do this well, you must educate people for music. Most only have an MTV education, poor and extremely manipulated by big corporations.

Try to find what is out there with quality and new, and try to select the next hit in advance, before everyone knows that it will be a hit. If you position yourself ahead of the charts, you're not following them.

Dave Clarke used the right words, when mentioning, "I may be established but I'll never be establishment".

ATTRACTING FOLLOWERS

Regarding profile pictures, you don't need many or too significant, but you do need original pictures with immediate impact, so that you may keep yourself more easily in the mind of those who find them.

Usually, in the music industry, this means pictures taken with famous DJs, hot girls and crowds of clubbers.

Remember that a popular DJ creates his own reputation and doesn't wait for others to give it to him, which won't actually happen. People only recognize what is already recognized, because they follow trends, they're just followers. So, your image has to be promoted ahead of any result, and, when those results come, they'll simply match it, without the need for any change or update.

Those who believe that reputation must be conquered, are usually anxiously hoping that someone may give them success in one day, out of nowhere. And, that's not likely to happen.

Over time, they develop a behavior similar to parasites, always trying to get their success by attaching themselves to successful people. That's not healthy or good for yourself and your artistic reputation.

Success may come when you least expect, but you should be prepared to receive it, and not fighting to get it by force.

Foremost, have fun and bring fun to your page! A DJ attracts people because he gives them something missing in daily life, and that's joy. People go to clubs to forget their daily problems and have fun, and a DJ is responsible for it.

More than providing atmospheres with similar musical tendencies to what they listen at home, you should be giving something new, a new world, where people can fully engage their imagination and feelings in, while having a break from their problems.

Also important to notice, is that your pictures must show something personal as well, like things you love, even your dog, your favorite moments, etc. Don't worry about having everyone following you, because that would be an unwise mistake. You want people that recognize you to follow you, so you shouldn't worry about those that criticize your work.

You can't force people to love your work, or even you. You can only expect to attract people that love the same things as you. Provide them with such opportunity, by inviting those with similar musical taste to your page. Find the DJs you like, people with the same musical preferences, the fans of the artists that you listen the most and offer them an opportunity to be added in your page.

This is how you make yourself visible. They'll see your page, comment on it, give appreciations, etc.

MANAGING FAME

From all the comments you receive, you should answer only to those that are positive, and merely with a simple "thank you".

Worse than your own management of fame, is how others handle it.

People tend to worship public figures as if they were gods, so don't expect a fan to talk to you as if you were a normal person, and be very careful about who you talk with, because some people are very evil. Many private conversations I had with some individuals, often replying to their own topic, allowed them to spread false rumors based on lies, things I never said and never happened.

Needless to say that after these experiences I started being more careful and acting like I should, like a famous person.

People can't handle a normal person that they believe to belong to another planet.

Don't feel pressured to correspond to what others want and don't be afraid to tell them that you don't have time for them! Be nice and kind to others, but very careful about what you write to them!

Once I had a very simple email, being blogged all over the place, simply because I was famous and those that were competing with me, decided to ask several people to contact me and pretend to be someone they were not. And, that's how insane some people can be.

As your popularity grows, you will receive more negative messages and notice more harmful websites and blogs. Don't read them! You can't fight it back, but they can affect you severely!

Creativity and negativity aren't good friends! If you try to fight back jealousy, you'll lose what makes you who you are. So, focus on the future and in what you're trying to accomplish! But, if the opportunity comes, don't be afraid to punch someone in the nose and get sued for it! Some do deserve it! Unless, they're just playing paparazzi with your photos, as that's a lost battle.

Sometimes I was asked about why I attacked some idiots. The answer is very simple: I felt better with myself.

The main point is that, if you're awakening feelings in others, for whatever reason it is, it means they feel threaten by you. Mocking your words and acts is just the only tool they have to bring you down from where you are already.

PEOPLE THAT SHOULDN'T PERFORM

Only those that aren't meaningful for society despise successful people, as they're afraid that their success may diminish even more their insignificance. It's a feeling related to survival instincts, which is more prominent in very uncreative and mentally disturbed individuals, despite their occupation during the day and what they seem to be.

Actually, the most unfriendly people I've ever met in the DJing world, were Engineers, Physicians, Soldiers, Psychologists and Psychiatrists during the day. And, ironically, the friendliest ones, were Teachers, Bus Drivers, Shop Owners and Employees from Restaurants, that decided to DJ to uplift their self-esteem.

I'm not talking about a rule here, but a tendency, proving that the most frustrated individuals seek to become DJs to escape their own reality, but don't play or behave like they truly are. And, maybe some jobs are prone to develop more stress, scorn and resentment than others.

Nevertheless, I found a better balance among Artists that have always been connected to Art or some form of expression in life, namely, individuals that love to sing, are photographers, are passionate for drawing and painting, or those working in the field of cinema.

Besides, my background as a music producer, has very likely prepared me better to become a DJ, than what I saw in many others that started DJing at home, without any other background in the field of art.

I've learned from experience that it's easier to teach an Artist to do art with music, than to explain to a Non-Artist the meaning of art in music.

BEING ATTACKED

Basically, and although weird, haters believe that your success may kill their chances of becoming anybody in society, and that's why some may become so aggressive that they can even send you death threat messages or try to attack you physically, as many did to me.

The only thing I could do about it was go to a police station and warn them that I might be killing someone soon in order to protect myself. Once my words were registered, I went on with my life normally. Not much more could I do about it.

Remember also that your first haters represent a training practice to what will come in the near future, as the most popular you get, the more haters you'll attract. The proportion isn't reasonable until you achieve a degree so high that bodyguards will open the way for you among the crowd and nobody has a chance to compete with you anymore.

In other words, you can't avoid your enemies; you can only overcome them with your success.

The number of real friends that you will make, DJs that support you without any jealousy, is extremely limited. I found two during all my life and they were actually both from very poor backgrounds.

Sometimes you'll find yourself lonely in your path to fame, and with much more haters than friends. But, if you keep your heart with you and you always do what you love to do, you'll have the strength needed to keep climbing the mountain of fame.

One way or another, soon you'll find that it's a difficult and hardworking path, and that's why it's not for anyone. Not everyone deserves to be famous, as it demands a very high price that only a few are willing to pay.

Nobody will be able to take your own achievements from you. You'll always know who you are and what you've accomplished. So, the amount of people hating you isn't as meaningful as the number of times you DJ in a famous club or have a song in a famous radio.

My enemies can hate me for playing music all over the world and being on MTV, as they'll never get that chance, but the fact is that they can't take those achievements from me either. So, hating is pointless and paying attention to them as well.

Whatever people may tell you, don't ever listen to criticism and critics! They're just people trying to be noticed through you, but they're actually not meaningful, unless they work for the music industry and are trying to help you reach their level.

Whatever happens, don't be afraid of fame, and don't be afraid to be refused and denied or criticized! Learn from your experiences, your failures and mistakes!

The less you expose yourself, the more others will be forced to criticize your work and not your personality. And, the criticism to your work, whether it's more or less true, can help you see what people think about your performances and adapt in your own way.

PRODUCTION AND PERFORMANCE

Having a proper image isn't enough for an artist, obviously. You need to present your work to the public! As a DJ, you must have several sets online, for anyone to download and listen!

The basic principle behind organizing yourself and promoting your work, matches exactly what you did when searching for music.

However, it's not a shame if you think you need DJ lessons in order to present a good job. Usually, DJ courses are led by professional DJs with years of experience, and it's always a good option to do them, even if you're simply updating and expanding your skills.

Paul Van Dyk has a very good principle to resume these paragraphs. He says: "I don't want to lead people, I want to tempt them, I want to create a new world for them, when they're losing themselves in my music. I want to inspire them".

Independently of how much you know or have to become a DJ, I'll enumerate the necessary steps before reaching fame:

* Do a DJ course and buy the turntable that fits you best, as each DJ has a different technique and preference when performing live;

* If you don't want to buy a turntable in the beginning, you can also download mixing software and learn to mix from your own computer;

* If you have no idea of what to do, mixing other sets can be a good start to practice, but make sure you're only mixing music from one specific genre, as the bpm will change when a set mixes genres.

The tendency nowadays is for DJs to use a computer and you won't easily find a turntable in an Asian Club, for example. Nevertheless, you can always carry your own DJ table, as most do.

Actually, carrying your own material is so commonly seen, that if you don't people will think you're an amateur, instead of seeing you as a professional, that can use any kind of material.

You don't need to worry much about the material, as it's mostly related to your technique when mixing. What really makes the difference is your quality as a DJ, the quality of your sound and your ability to play music that people enjoy listening and will make them talk about you in the following days.

MIXING WITH A COMPUTER

Personally, I don't like using computers to mix music, because although they do everything automatically, such as finding the right pitch for each track and matching them together instantaneously, they also do mistakes by default, such as confusing beats with bass. And, if this happens, it's not easy to control the problem and avoid noticeable breaks.

Another problem with computers, is that they make it easier to do silly mistakes, like pressing the wrong button by accident. And, this situation, even though it can merely ruin a set when mixing at home, can ruin a party when mixing live.

Computers are useful for what I call homework. It means, preparing your sets in advance and organize your CDs to play later in the party, or help with sound effects and sound quality, when remixing a track.

However, for this purpose, I would recommend software for music production, instead of virtual DJ tables.

One of the biggest advantages in using computers in a party is that it can help you significantly to improve the sound quality, and even replace other materials that often lack in live events.

PREPARING SETS FOR PARTIES

There are many ways to prepare yourself for a live event and, despite what other DJs may tell you, there's really no limit to what you can or can't do. It all depends on your intention and how you interpret DJing.

In my case, I like to create small sets of about 10 to 15 minutes each. And, the reason is that I don't see a performance as just playing music. It's more than that. I want to engage people in an experience of sound, which may include more than just music.

It's easier, for example, to prepare a mix of classical music and Opera with Hardstyle before an event, or combine a remix with voices from movies, to transmit a certain message, that you want to convey in your performance.

Once this is done, you can focus in mixing all these small sets, depending on how the occasion presents itself. Maybe you won't play one or two of them, but still make a great demonstration of what you want to show. This is more than just playing music; it's doing art through sound.

What people think about, regarding what a DJ should or shouldn't do, depends merely on their idea of what is the DJ's role, and that's why I always refused to perform in places where I don't have enough autonomy to play whatever I want.

Being a DJ is a job, but a DJ is not serving beer in a bar; he's a performer, an artist. Or, at least, he should be.

Other advantages related to preparing mixes in advance is that they save you moments in which you have to mix music live. You don't need to do this all the time, and, as a matter of fact, you should know how to create good breaks during your performances. Armin Van Buuren is one of the best examples on how to do this well.

If you like to produce music, it's wise to mix live as if you were producing, as this allows you to complement one activity with the other, while improving your results in both.

It's a fact that my work as a DJ was significantly improved by my experience as a producer, but the experience in DJing affected the way I create music positively.

Preparing mixes before a party also allows you to play more with live effects.

Everything you can do to be more unique, must be welcome within your creative thoughts and performances. Don't be afraid to be yourself and express your own personality! Your character in the sound used defines who you are as a DJ, your Artistic personality.

There's no need as well to take risks live, such as when mixing metal with techno. Besides, too much focus in mixing certain sounds will lead you to stop seeing the whole purpose of the performance.

Some seconds can't define one hour of show, and you only have two hands to apply any and all the ideas coming to your mind.

Make sure that these prepared sets have a coherent and easily followed style!

PRINCIPLES TO CREATE A GOOD SET

The key to create a good set is this: People like to be surprised within their expectations. And, that's why you should want to play in clubs where you'll likely be welcomed.

Make sure that your set is like a story that you're telling others. Any story is good, either it expresses romantic emotions, anger or sadness, as long as you insist in the main feeling behind it. Armin Van Buuren, Delerium, Tiesto and Paul Van Dyk are among the best storytellers in the music industry.

Express yourself with your music, be honest, be yourself and show your soul, by mixing according to how you feel in live.

I used to focus on my experiences to create completely different sets, always with quality. They included anger, sadness and happiness.

All you need to do is focus in your daily life and your emotions while creating the set. The more you can concentrate on those feelings while working and expressing yourself, the more the result will be faithful to your personality and demonstrate character.

Some musicians say that music is like a therapy and some psychologists also use it as a therapy due to this reason.

When creating music, you, as a producer or DJ, among many things, also learn and gain insights about yourself and your purpose in life. And, that means that people listening to your work will identify more easily with you, give you value for being honest, appreciate your honesty, appreciate your work and give you credit for expressing in a way that only a few can.

Those few are the most popular and that's what you'll become by training your quality in such way, while showing truthfulness and professionalism.

COMMITTING TO YOUR VALUES

Whatever you do, be yourself, and don't feel forced to play a particular style of music or genre.

It is a common characteristic in the biography of most famous musicians that, during the first years of their musical career, where rejected and ridiculed, while struggling to maintain their own identity and believes.

Marilyn Manson and Metallica have some of the most beautiful rock ballads ever and they didn't lose social respect because of that. In fact, by being honest to themselves, their words and feelings, people just respected them more and gave them more credit and value. But, their attitude has always been the same, even though in the beginning the feedback of the audience was quite different.

People will always change what they think about you according to their own judgment, so it's not wise to try to understand them. If you do need feedback, ask famous musicians for that, because they will more likely be honest with you, but if you need recognition, then ask yourself what are you really doing and what for.

Instead of the least experienced DJs, bringing lots of bags with CDs and Vinyl's every time they go perform, or the ones spending days closed at home preparing for an event, terribly scared of failing, you should be doing your homework regularly, as it will guarantee your quality later.

Professional DJs take their work seriously, by training their emotions first, before showing them live. Sound is just a tool within this method.

THE IMPORTANCE OF HOMEWORK

The experience you may have as a DJ isn't different from what you face in school. The ones that always do their homework are ready for the final exam and will pass it with high grades, if they're dedicated.

It's no surprise to see that, among the best World DJs, we can actually find many with college degrees. Even though one thing doesn't imply the other, the best DJs I've ever met in my life had college degrees in various fields, from Education to Engineering.

The lazy ones, dedicated themselves to a job they can do, in order not to feel too stupid to learn. And, sadly, the truth is that in life the same rules always apply, including in the music business. Those that do homework have more success and those that aren't afraid to learn go beyond their wildest dreams and expectations.

I'm probably a good example of the latest, as, interestingly, while most DJs believe I didn't deserve to be on MTV, they forget the fact I studied music on my own, every single night, for one entire year, instead of sleeping. I researched about basic concepts related to building a good song, I read biographies of DJs and took special attention to their words of advice, and I never wasted any opportunity to talk to other musicians, from any field, to understand their points of view about music.

I can't play a guitar or piano, but I worked very hard to deserve the victory I eventually accomplished. So, this leads me to give you a special advice if you want to be among the best: don't hate them for what they have! Appreciate them for what you can learn from them! You have much more to gain by being their friend!

RECOGNIZING FRIENDSHIPS

In 2013, Portugal had one DJ among the Top 100 world, named Pete Tha Zouk and, in 2014, they had another, named Diego Miranda. If you go to their website, you can see parties in which they're hugging each other, while describing themselves as great friends.

That's the true spirit in being great. You don't choose to be great; you make yourself great with your attitude to life and fame!

Nothing is forever, except what you allow yourself to experience. So, the friends you make and the people you learn from, are more important than any of your achievements.

I've helped many people win competitions, from music competitions to even speech competitions, and they all told me the same: what they've learn from me is far beyond what they got from their victory. On another hand, it's because they can recognize this that they won.

I wouldn't go so far, if I wasn't able to be thankful for the support I received from many Artists and Musicians cooperating with me.

If you want to be successful, you need to deserve it first, by building your success from within! You need to be positive and treasure the moments you have with others!

BEING DIFFERENT FROM THE REST

Those that don't know what makes a musician successful, are usually only good when being lucky. They don't know why they're good and lose such fame rather quickly, as they also don't know how to maintain it and keep it.

The best are very confident in what they do, to a point in which they tend to do things differently.

Experience showed me that the most popular DJs tend to bring a hand of CDs to parties as they know exactly what they want to do, while it is the least experienced DJ that always brings more music.

I remember one night in which I was standing in a circle with all the team I was going to play with that night. We were 9 DJs and the party was going to start in thirty minutes. As we looked at each other, one asked the others about how many CDs they brought with them. All answered with a smile while showing their bag packed with music. But, then they asked the most popular in the group, which was me, how much music I brought, as they didn't saw my backpack and were surprised about that.

I was ashamed to answer and make everyone feel embarrassed, so I simply answered: "Not as much as you". However, one of them, the most experienced, with 40 years of a background playing music throughout Europe, interrupted me to say, while reaching for his pocket: "I only have these 2 CDs."

At this point, I laughed and reached for my pocket to answer, "me too".

Everyone, except both of us, was astonished, not knowing what to say.

The most popular and the most experienced, brought both less music than anyone else.

We were very confident about what to do that night. And, both of us prepared well our homework. In each CD, we had enough music for a forty minutes performance, but we really didn't need so much time, as we just wanted to show our quality and uniqueness.

Although it was just a coincidence, we both had prepared in advance several remixes and effects, along with the music we had brought, to bring people something new and different to experience.

The fact is that we were the only ones that had dedicated hours in preparing for that event. Those CDs were merely a resume of our dedication, a conclusive idea of what we intended to do.

This event was a huge success but, in the next days, people only spoke about the two of us.

We were unique and different from the rest. I mixed voices from war movies and politicians, with Operas, Classical music and Buddhist mantras, among other unexpected things, while playing Techno, Industrial and Hardstyle. And, my senior friend, mixed classic oldies and samples from the 70s, with Hardstyle and Techno, along with several uplifting effects during the performance.

It was all very wild and new to everyone, including the DJs and Clubbers. It was one of the most original Rave parties ever made.

That, I believe, clarifies the difference between showing art and playing music.

The other DJs were also very good, but nobody remembered them after the party. Everyone described the event as a party with 9 DJs, in which one of them played amazing effects mixed with oldies, and the other mixed Hardstyle tracks that nobody ever heard before with religious sounds and Operas.

This experience shows basically that, being the best you can be in the right moment and place, are the ingredients to become successful as a DJ in a certain party.

People used to go to parties to "have a great time and to forget their troubles and worries and stresses of the week and enjoy themselves, and I think that the music was a huge, important part of that" (Paul Oakenfold).

CHOOSING A CLUB

The places where you choose to play represent the beginning of your reputation as a DJ. They lead you to adjust what is played to the audience, while building your name among certain groups.

If you choose a place that you don't like, due to lack of options, you'll continue to lack opportunities to grow in the future. But, such places will also take away your passion for music and DJing.

You need to research on the internet first, and then go out with friends to clubs that you believe to be potentially suitable for you!

Don't give your sets to anyone! Make sure first that the atmosphere of the nightclubs you visit match your personality and that you can do a good job in that club, preferably, better than the one of those playing there.

You should visit as many clubs as possible before finding the one that fits you.

Ask yourself how you feel in all the clubs visited, while checking if you can identify with the clubbers in those places. And, in the end, choose one you identify the most with.

Don't be afraid to choose a bar or club that is barely known to others, because it may represent a good start. Most famous Clubs were unknown, until famous DJs decided to play there.

An unknown club allows you more freedom to set a trend. And, this trend will be related to your style.

Other options to take into consideration are the recently open clubs and those that don't have a particular musical style yet. Truth is, most club managers have no idea about what music they want or what music their club should play. And, that allowed me to easily change many musical tendencies in several nightclubs.

Basically speaking, everyone wants to have fun, in an original and peaceful environment. So, if you can do it, you'll be welcomed.

You can also search for opportunities in small events, or where the music isn't chosen yet, such as private parties and students' festivals Most of the DJs I've met started here.

It's also easy to start your reputation by playing in your friend's parties. I've started like this, by being invited to play in private parties and later for bigger events. The first party had 200 people, but the second had 3000.

APPLYING AS A DJ

When finding the ideal place to play, the nightclub where you feel that you can contribute in bringing a new level of experience to people and show something more original and interesting, propose yourself to play there! Simply walk to the bar and ask to talk to the manager, or ask for the manager's contact! Then, contact him or talk to him directly!

You just need to say that you're a DJ and then ask for permission to play in the less crowded night as a trial, for free or half the payment.

Mention that you just want to show your quality, while clarifying that he has nothing to lose with you!

Club managers and owners are usually more open-minded than most people, especially if they too are DJs or have a DJing background. But, there's nothing to lose in asking to organizers of events if you can play in their parties too. You can just send them a simple email with your requested fee and links to your sets online.

Don't be afraid to start from zero, as you can always build your way from there.

Whatever you do, don't just play music! Try to know the people around you, make friends with the team, ask their opinions regarding your performance and see if you can be invited more often!

Nevertheless, be patient, because in the field of music nobody is ever sure about nothing, and you shouldn't pressure people to get what you want!

Applying for an opportunity as DJ is like seducing women, in the sense that you can't chase and look needy. You need to go to as many clubs as possible and find one that matches you the most, either by identifying with the manager or the environment.

NEGOTIATING YOUR PRICE

Before thinking about money or settling with a job as DJ, make sure you're respected and people around you can recognize your value, as you're as worth as what others think about you, and you won't be able to do much about it thereafter.

Due to the immense amount of DJs without any quality, there are many stereotypes about how a DJ should look like and behave, and, unfortunately, they're associated with this kind of people. So, the tendency, as you grow in the business, is to find more places where you're not respected and accepted. And, that's why you should be active in pursuing a place that can fit you inside as a DJ of the house, instead of planning a tour around the world.

In conversation with very experienced DJs, I came to the conclusion that those investing in building their reputation in a particular place, grown faster than the ones traveling around the world.

Most DJs choose the south of Spain to settle down but, generally speaking, there are many more places where you can do this. However, I wouldn't advise most Asian countries, like China, Malaysia or Philippines, because people have a very low sense of mutual respect and musical culture in these places, unless, you apply to work under a one year contract minimum.

The salary is often good, but you'll be playing hits most of the times and you'll need to make an extra effort in researching local tendencies in music.

As for what people think about how a DJ should look like, you just have to do, what you shouldn't actually do, to be accepted. That includes having the face of someone that woke up in the afternoon, not shaving, having a peculiar hairstyle, and bringing two bags full of CDs in your back like a camel.

The dumber people are, the more these stereotypes apply, so it all depends in how much you really want to be a DJ. Sometimes you may need to pretend to be someone you're not just to get a chance to show who you really are.

When choosing a residence to become a DJ there, make sure you can grow and learn in that place, instead of just being forced to play music you don't really like.

PROMOTING YOURSELF

A DJ shouldn't behave like a prostitute, just playing music to give pleasure to others and get money from it. You must develop a path as a DJ, and make sure you can learn from each night you perform.

Those nights will give you feedback to what you've been doing, so if you have a plan it's easier to self-analyze your work. And, this plan must always include music you love to play.

You should always carry a business card with you as well, mentioning your website and contact number! And, you should offer it to those you meet, so that they may remember you and listen to your music afterwords!

The majority of the parties where I was invited to play, came with invitations from people I've never met and that got my contact from somebody else.

People like to recommend DJs in whom they trust and believe to be professional. Therefore, your friends are probably the best sources to recommend you, and, as a DJ, you should make friends in your parties, because people will approach you if they like your performance.

Those that approach you are like business cards, because they'll talk about you to others. Usually, this happens with the opposite gender, so offer them your business card in those moments, so that they can show it to their friends!

Remember that most people inviting you are focusing in how you make them feel, rather than your music style, which very often they don't know anything about.

MAKING FRIENDS

If you're too self-centered and antisocial, people won't feel comfortable near you, and won't feel the need to come back just to listen you perform.

As a DJ, you must make people feel good in your presence as well!

I always dedicated myself to make friends in my parties and, many times, I completely abandoned my DJ table, to talk to clubbers in the dancefloor and dance with them to my own music.

This is one of the most memorable and enjoyable experiences in being a DJ. Nothing beats dancing to your own music, with your own fans. It's an amazing sensation, much higher than being on drugs or seeing people dance from your upper position on stage.

It's also common, especially if you don't open yourself as mentioned above, that people may want to approach you, and even enter your space. And, this is a particularly sensitive moment, for many reasons.

Most professional DJs want to be positioned in a stage, or surrounded by security guards, not to be bothered during their performance. But, being distant from the ones dancing isn't a good way to do things, unless it's a major event with millions of attendants.

The smaller the party, the more you need to be in contact with your fans. But, when they invade your space, with their drinks just above your CDs and turntable, the alarm should be ringing in your head.

Most people are unaware of what they do, and can easily push a button by accident. So, you should make sure they don't come too close to you during a performance, which will definitely be difficult to accomplish, since they can't hear you from where they are.

If you tell them to wait, they may also not react very well, as they can't understand why. And, that's why you have to manage these situations well.

It's a kind of a double job, socializing and DJing at the same time, but good energy follows positive vibes, and that's how you build your karma and image in the music industry.

BEING IN DANGER

My reputation wasn't built only with music, but also with a positive attitude and friendly approach, both towards DJs and fans. They enjoyed feeling respected and part of my world, without distinctions.

However, you can't make everyone happy. Those that felt threatened by my presence, spent hours imagining things to trash my name and reputation.

They would also send their own "spies" to collect information about me and then gossip furthermore, in a constant attempt to damage my name and events.

Destroying and taking my posters out of the walls where they were being advertised wasn't enough. During this time, I received several dead threats, anonymous messages in my email box and suffered multiple attempts to hacker my email account, MySpace page and others.

I lost my webpage, which was completely deleted, and I lost my artistic email account, which was on Hotmail, as well as my Myspace account, among others. And, I was never able to recover them since, as all my messages to the administrators of these websites keep being ignored.

In other words, whenever you see "Genius Deejay", is not me anymore, even though the picture is the same, the music is the same, and all the rest didn't change.

Dan Van Casteele is my only real artistic name for the moment.

HIRING SECURITY GUARDS

At some point, I didn't have a choice, but to hire security guards to come with me every time I was performing, because it's impossible to focus on your music and in the psychos that may be among the public. You don't want to be surprised by a bottle in your head or a knife in your back. And, that's how cowards usually attack.

My background in martial arts wouldn't help me if I wasn't paying attention, and you can't do so many things at the same time, especially in a nightclub, with such a low visibility.

So, next time someone tells you that your payment is too high, you can tell them that you need to hire security guards, because the more famous you become the more psychos you'll have around you, imagining things that never happened, just to excuse themselves from hitting you.

This is particularly likely to happen if their friends like your music, and even more if they are musicians themselves.

There's too much insanity in our society nowadays, so it's easier to find these groups than healthier ones.

As a matter of fact, one of the individuals mentioned above was the Psychiatrist I talked about in the first chapters.

You need to be very careful about what you say and do! The more you react, the more they boost their ego, because these nobodies are essentially struggling for attention.

I couldn't afford more than two to three security guards to come with me, but ironically, the more security guards you have the more important people think you are. So, one thing leads to another, and having a group of strong men protecting you actually increases your reputation as a famous DJ.

REPLYING TO INVITATIONS

When invitations come, always say yes, without hesitation or questions about it. You can always talk about the details later.

Prepare yourself to any incoming event with different music genres that you enjoy playing and simply be who you are. Those that invite you aren't expecting anything more than what they already know about you. And, if things don't work well, don't worry much about it, as all experiences are good experiences. They represent opportunities to learn.

At least, you'll learn more about the people that invite you, how to judge a party and know what to expect from it. But, if you have to say no, do it later and for a good reason that can be easily acceptable, such as:

"I have a better proposal for the same day".

And, if this isn't true and people find out, you can simply say:

"They canceled the event in the last minute for security reasons".

As a professional DJ, you must always know what to say in the right moment without being afraid to say no or yes.

That's how the music industry works, because everyone needs to be strategical about their options, without damaging their reputation or the work of others.

THE WORSE THING DJS DO

Never, ever, quit an event in the last minute!

I had many DJs doing this to me, and I really trashed them on the phone with the worse things I could remember saying to someone. It's simply the most unprofessional thing to do, for whatever reason.

Some, for unknown reasons, would simply disappear just 5 minutes before their performance.

You should never work with someone like this or trust them even as friends!

A DJ commits to his words and, if he doesn't, he shouldn't deserve any chance ever again.

You should never refuse a party in a moment in which it can compromise the team organizing it. If you want to make a quick decision, always say yes, when the event matches your musical style, and say no when it doesn't.

This is how professional DJs think and behave, and how you should things do as well.

KEEPING YOUR FANS

People that want to be the best everywhere and push too much the boundaries of what they can do, will end up destroying their reputation, if not with the Clubs, with their friends. And, those friends are your first and forever biggest fans. If you lose them, you'll have to rebuild yourself from scratch.

I've made many DJs famous with my events and reputation, and I told them how to maintain it. But, most didn't learn the lesson well and focused too much in their own ego. So, gradually, they lost everyone and their parties started to be completely empty.

If you're doing the right thing, your parties will increasingly have more people every time you perform. But, you need experience to know how to apply these principles, while being respectful to others. And, this is something most DJs I've met couldn't understand, when seeing the amount of people I was bringing to my events.

My name wasn't just associated with good music, but also with good personality and respect towards everyone working with me. It's a basic and vital criteria to judge people in the music industry.

I wouldn't mind, for example, to cut my performance by half in order to give more time to another DJ performing in my party, if he was doing a very good job, and I actually did this many times.

PREPARING FOR A PERFORMANCE

Before your performance, ask questions to someone that knows who is going to attend your party, regarding what kind of people usually come and what kind of clubbers you should be expecting, as well as the kind of music DJs usually play there!

Further conclusions should be made by your own observations. But, visit the place at least one time before your show, check the music played, the kind of people that are there, what people dance to and what makes the dance floor emptier.

Prepare yourself well, so that you "don't do what you've heard, do what you think you gonna hear" (Dennis Ferrer).

Analyze the quality of the DJs playing there before your event with a critical thinking and see what you could do better than them. Remember that this is what will make the difference and increase your value.

Also, make sure to analyze the sounds of the music being played, as usually it isn't as much about the genres being played as it is about the similarity in tendencies.

It's based on this principle that I was able to be accepted in a heavy metal nightclub, with Hardstyle and Techno.

Nevertheless, I was careful enough to smooth the gap, by playing Gothic and guitar samples with Darkcore, Industrial and Gothcore.

Whatever you do, remember that your influence must be positive, rather than forced. Clubbers can feel the difference when a DJ is pushing something they don't want, but they're also open to styles that can go beyond their expectations.

DEALING WITH INCOMPATIBILITY

Imagining that you enjoy Techno, but the place where you're going to perform regularly only plays Pop, you must bring some Pop music with you, in order to make your entrance less aggressive to the audience, what would lead them to abandon the club immediately upon arrival.

Nevertheless, don't just give people what they want, otherwise you'll have more difficulties to mix your way into your own style, in this case Techno.

One way to do this, consists in preparing some remixes of Techno with Pop, as well as techno tracks that match the samples used in the Pop songs you're planning to use.

In order to do this job well, you must take into consideration the sounds used in all the Techno and Pop tracks you're willing to use. Then, as you prepare your set, you must divide it into 3 sections:

* The first is related to what people want;

* The second is about your own work to help them accept what you'll do in the third part;

* The last section is about what you really want to do.

The overall time should include about 3 songs for the first part, 3 more in the second, and the rest being up to you.

Depending on the total amount of time for your performance, you may need to prepare backups, consisting, in this situation, of more than 3 Pop songs that you'll be playing every time people get bored with Techno.

You must see yourself as a coach that is training people that usually don't like Techno, to listen to it and appreciate it.

You can't force people to like Techno, but you can teach them to respect it, if you play music that they can accept. That's how I made Pop fans appreciate Techno. And, in the end, they kept asking me about the music played in the party, which was the same I wanted to play.

People must learn to appreciate different music, and appreciate your work as well, and in order to do this, you have to teach those that are often brainwashed by what they listen on radio and TV.

The DJ is also and above all, a pedagogue of sound and music.

DJING STYLES

There are three types of DJs:

* One thinks about his performance as a linear experience, in which he can pretty much play the same tone from beginning to end;

* The other sees his performance as a progressive experience, in which he can increase the quality, the speed of his songs or even the variety, during his performance;

*Finally, the third type is the rarer, and is the Organic DJ. He doesn't do what he wants or what others ask for, but what he feels.

The Organic DJ is the one that will completely stop the sound in the dancefloor, just to get some attention to his work, when people are dancing randomly. He's also the one that will play with the voices of his songs, simply because he wants to have fun, and the one that will play with the turntable during his performance, instead of simply playing music.

In other words, the Organic DJ is also a rebel. He doesn't care about what people think about him, because he isn't struggling to be accepted. He wants people to remember him, one way or another, either they love him or hate him.

He will do what he feels that he should, simply because he wants to.

THE ORGANIC DJ

This type of DJ is more sensitive to his environment, therefore, he adjusts to his experience and the people around him, but always in a way that positions him as the leader of what's happening.

He, basically, controls the whole dance floor with his attitude.

There are very few DJs with this ability, but we can find them among the best. They are the ones that do what we couldn't predict but, yet, make us feel excited with their performance. And, some of the best examples are probably Carl Cox and Fat Boy Slim.

Nevertheless, they can also adapt to other types of DJing. And, when doing a progressive performance, for example, they'll use many techniques to increase addiction in their listeners.

The basic principle consists in not following the audience, but make the audience follow you instead. Therefore, by combining the organic with the progressive style, it means you'll only proceed with a particular style when the audience is in your hands. This, because, when you feel them slipping away, you have to catch them back with something else.

A DJ must act like a seducer! You can't just rape people's hears with your sound; you must seduce them to your world of music!

Look at your audience and think: "I'm going to make love to every single one of you" (Erick Morillo)!

Give first to the audience what they want, in order to bring them afterward to your side! Then, gradually, teach them about your own way of playing music, until they can understand it!

When DJing in a Gothic Club, for example, I played samples from vampire movies, along with Gothic bands, and then samples from Gothic music with Techno. Finally, I took it from there, when everyone was on the mood, and pushed it to a more aggressive Hardcore sound.

Merely two hours later, you could see Gothics in a rave party of electronic sounds. And, I guess most didn't even realized how it happened, as some approached me to say:

"I usually hate electronic music, but your performance was awesome".

EQUALIZING RHYTHMS

Playing music is like surfing; a small wave is usually followed by a bigger one. So, you must understand this principle in order to apply it to your performances.

Here are some examples:

* You can't play the same style of music for more than fifteen to twenty minutes, without creating a break or another kind of change in the sequence, as this tends to be the amount of time people usually tolerate before feeling bored;

* You must create your own waves within the sets, by changing style or sounds after each break;

* Stronger and longer reactions demand deeper and quieter breaks, so a mix of Hard-style music matches perfectly with Opera and Classical music, as much as Techno matches with Gothic music, and House music matches with New Age. You'll notice that the most famous DJs have got their insight on this already;

* The emotional reaction of your audience must match the music you're playing, so make sure that they're not out of tune. Most DJs are so concentrated in the music they want to play, that they don't really see what's happening in the dance floor.

EVALUATING YOUR WORK

What you see in the dancefloor matches what you're doing. Therefore, pay attention, in particular, to the following:

* Every time someone shouts with joy, it's like you're reaching the pick of your performance. It won't last lost, so don't abuse it!

If people are really enjoying a lot your show, you have about 5 to 10 minutes after this shout before the dancefloor dies. So, you have to change music and create a break with some Chillout sounds or voices without beats, after a while.

DJs that try to keep the same style, just because people are enjoying it, kill the moment by insisting in this repetition.

* Notice the most extroverted or drunk dancers, as they tend to set the tendency in the public!

Usually, you see a crazy guy alone, in the middle of the dancefloor, having fun on his own, but soon after you see a bunch of people around him, doing the same. So, whatever you do, make sure these guys are always happy!

* Try to interpret the emotions in the dancefloor!

People want to dance for different reasons, and you must be able to detect them. Your music should allow them to express their emotions. And, as music is mostly about communicating emotions, you must choose always the one that matches your audience the most;

* Whatever happens in the dancefloor, you must always be struggling to uplift your audience!

You can't call yourself a good DJ if people fight with each other in your performances.

I've seen it a lot with other DJs, but it has never happen to me. Basically, your job must be focused in making people feel more relaxed, united and happy.

The best DJs make people feel so uplifted that they suddenly start dancing with each other, without any introduction, communication or presentation whatsoever. It has happen to me as a clubber and as a DJ.

I have no doubt that this is a requirement all DJs should have in mind. It's nice to have a shirt saying "music against racism", but it's nicer to see people of different backgrounds, that didn't knew each other before the event, hugging, dancing and jumping together to your sounds.

THE SPIRITUAL ART IN DJING

A DJ is like a priest of the modern era. He must know how make people feel enlightened, united and spiritual, with the sound of his music.

In ancient times, we would sing healing mantras in a way that could touch our heart and soul, while playing musical instruments.

The purpose hasn't changed and that's why, before each of my performances, I used to ear tribal music from Native Americans, to inspire my performance that night.

People must have faith in you in order to follow you, so don't ruin their expectations of enjoying a great night in your presence! Believe in what you're doing and allow them to enjoy as well, with as many techniques and sound effects as necessary!

You must believe first in your love for the art of DJing, before others can see it and you must create your own path in which later others will eventually follow!

People must enjoy and "listen without taking drugs... feel the emotions in it...get on another level without the drugs" (Tiesto).

CONTROLLING A PERFORMANCE

The less experience you have as a DJ, the more techniques you need to camouflage your mistakes in a way that nobody notices. And, these are some of the ways to do it:

* When doing a mistake, don't pretend it didn't happen! Instead, repeat it three more times, and pretend it was all part of the music.

All mistakes can be repeated, if you know how and have the right timing, and that's how you make your performance sound perfect.

* Avoid doing serious mistakes when mixing, by keeping a constant bpm throughout a small set and before a break without beats!

* Don't be unpredictable with the speed of your music, or people will have difficulties to catch up! Instead, increase it gradually, or after a break between songs!

* Follow the 3/7 rule, for higher success with the clubbers, which is 127.3 bpm for house, 133.7 for trance, 137.3 for Techno and 147.3 for Hardtech!

The best sets you'll ever hear, and the most famous DJs, in any style, all follow this rule.

*Allow people to rest, so that they don't abandon the dancefloor, or get bored with the music!

You can do this by changing the emotions transmitted in the music, for example, between happiness to monotony, or between sadness to anger. It's something like using commercials during a movie, so that nobody falls asleep before the set ends.

You can also do this with breaks composed of environmental music, voice samples or whatever your imagination and ideas taken from other DJs you admire may inspire you to do.

* If your mix is going very bad and you can't catch up with the pitch of the music being played, simply find the right moment and take all the beats off the music being displayed. You can more easily mix without beats.

In fact, anyone can DJ without previous experience, by using this technique. You can do this by pressing the bass button to zero.

However, you may want to regulate it well, before your performance, so that it may work as you expect.

The art of DJing consists also in doing all of what was mentioned in a way that nobody can see it. You must be subtle, fast and have the right and proper timing during your work.

Mixing well, knowing how to use sound effects and having a good timing, are all important skills that you must learn to master with proper training on your own.

You can prepare a CD of sound effects to help you in those moments and keep it prepared next to you when mixing live.

STRATEGIES ON STAGE

As most clubs are merely equipped with one turntable of double deck, the ideal thing to do before a performance would be plugging your computer to the table for sound effects or plug a second mixer, in order to have four decks to play with at the same time, which can be needed for effects and breaks between sets.

The most professional DJs do this and I started doing it as well, more than 10 years ago, but everyone criticized me. People are, generally speaking, very short minded, so it's ironic to see that nowadays things have went from one extreme to another, and most modern DJs don't even use decks anymore; they simply mix mp3s.

We're living in a totally new generation with different perspectives about music.

Actually, this strategy will apply in many different combined hypotheses, but you'll always face rejection and criticism when doing something different and not understood, even though 10 years later everyone may be doing the same.

You can combine many materials, in fact. It all depends on what you want to do, but practice first on your own, so that you don't take unnecessary risks during your performance!

SIMPLE WAYS TO MIX

You should use two decks to mix and other two for samples and special effects. And, if you're too afraid to mix the beats, due to lack of experience, know that you don't have to. You don't have to do it all the time and you also don't have to do it at all.

A DJ is an art performer and not a pitch-master, as many believe. You don't even have to know how to scratch vinyl to be named DJ.

It's only natural that those that have followed a longer and harder path may feel jealous and angry for those that reach the same goals quicker. But, that shouldn't stop you from continuing in the fastest path.

The main thing to keep in mind, is the goal you have and the reason why you want to DJ. The rest, must be seen as merely personal DJing techniques and you should only take into consideration the ones that match your DJing style of playing music.

If you don't want to mix beats when playing live, prepare sets at home of fifteen minutes each that start and end without bass. And, every time you finish one of those sets, you can simply put the next one without any hard work or mixing.

The strategy here consists in focusing in your small 15 minutes sets to mix, instead of 3 minutes tracks.

However, even though this may make your job easier, you shouldn't be lazy about it. You can take advantage of this technique to focus more on others that can improve your performance, namely, sound effects and voice samples from movies to be played at the same time.

You can also improve the effect of your performance if you control part of the work as a VJ.

Other things you can do, consist in playing more with the turntable, such as, taking the bass off in crucial moments, and increasing the mediums and lows in others, depending on what you're playing.

WORKING WITH OTHERS

You don't have to do all the work on your own or even experience things alone. Invite your friends to come to your parties for emotional support, even if you're not playing their musical style!

If you have a friend that wants to help you in the DJing part, invite him as well, as your backup to help you during the performance! And, if you have a friend that would like to DJ, give him a chance to play during your performance for a few minutes!

The same applies to other friends that are DJs, as you can invite them to play with you in a team.

It's always easier to play with others than alone and it helps in promoting your image as well. Besides, two people playing together bring different ideas at the same time to the performance, which means more ideas and styles mixing with the dancefloor and, therefore, quicker success.

Your friends are also your best advisers. They'll tell you immediately if the party is working or not and what others in the dancefloor are thinking, so that you know beforehand what to do.

HAVING FUN

You can and should organize your own parties. If you have a place, either an apartment, garage or house in the countryside, use it!

The same applies if you know a nightclub that is closed in certain days of the week, as you can offer yourself to create a party there, once every six months or every three months.

Start by smaller clubs, as they're easy to fill with guests!

I mentioned three months, because you'll need plenty of time to promote it online, create posters and distribute them in music shops and colleges.

If you have a place with all the necessary sound equipment is much better. Otherwise, you can only do small parties for closest friends.

The more people attend your parties, the more potent your sound has to be, which demands for more expensive material.

These experiences will help you enhance your trust in your own work and in yourself as a DJ. They provide a safe practice for all the advices and techniques mentioned in this book.

INVITING OTHER DJS

Always invite one of the club DJs, where you're suppose to perform, to your performance, to make sure the DJs in the Club feel comfortable with your presence, but also to receive advices from them for that specific night!

You can also put an advertisement online. There are lots of amateur DJs that would love to have an opportunity to play, even for free, just to show their value. And, the most honorable thing you can do as a DJ, is to invite them to play with you.

It's a very fulfilling attitude that allows you to make friends with other DJs, while releasing yourself from any egocentric attitudes that being a DJ can bring.

These DJs may also invite you later to their parties, which creates a network of opportunities for everyone.

You should offer them a percentage of the profits or tell them upfront if you can't pay in the first event, as they're just showing their work and you don't expect to earn money from it.

If they accept the deal is on, otherwise, respect their decision!

EVALUATING A DJ

To know if a DJ is good enough, the basic way to evaluate consists in listening to their set.

However, with so much information online, it's wiser to know all you can in a few minutes, by listening to different sets, read comments of people on their webpages, etc.

Other basic rules to evaluate them, consist in the following:

* Make sure they have experience in playing more than one musical style!

* If that DJ is going to perform with you, make sure his style matches yours, as it shouldn't be the same, but must complement your performance with something you can't do!

For example, if I play Hardstyle, I would want to invite a DJ that plays Psytrance. These styles complement each other, make the event more interesting and attract much more people that are willing to see two DJs playing these styles.

* Make sure the DJ you invite can bring many people with him as, in the end, an event is seen as successful depending on the marketing applied and number of people attending.

REASONS TO ORGANIZE LINE-UPS

If you have enough time, don't play alone! Invite as many DJs as you can, and allow each to play between 30 minutes to one hour only!

Parties with many DJs attract much more people. Besides, DJs must see them as opportunities to advertise themselves, and not truly to express their work, which should happen only when they have more time to perform and less competition.

In a party with many DJs, you can be the last one, which will help you gain more attention. Everyone will understand it, if you're the one organizing the event, while giving them an opportunity to play with you.

But, not many DJs understand that when they're invited to perform, they're actually being offered a chance to advertise themselves. Many see it arrogantly and are greedy in their requests, losing an opportunity to show how much they're worth, which helps them gain more attention and make friends.

Being a DJ in an event with many, is mostly an experience that you should never refuse, even when requested to play for free!

If you love music, you understand why. But, not many DJs are mature enough to see things in this way.

Most of the times people don't go to an event so much for the names seen on a poster, but mostly to listen to a guaranteed diversity in music. And, that's the guarantee that a party with many DJs offers, so people don't really care about how long each performs, because they know that every 30 minutes something else will be heard, which makes the night less boring, while enhancing curiosity.

The more curious people are, the more open minded they become about the performers, and that's a big advantage for the DJs, that can play more freely, without common restrictions.

SHARING YOUR MEMORIES

Create memories of your parties by taking as many pictures as possible and creating as many movies as you can, especially, movies of your performances and highlights!

With those videos and pictures, you can create great posts on your websites and let people know more about you.

As you post these images and videos online, more people will contact you. And, everyone that does it is a potential fan. Therefore, make sure you have their contacts to promote your future performances online. It's much easier and faster.

You can start by creating a list of emails of people that contacted you, in order to let them know about your parties. But, not only that, as you can organize dinners before the events with all your closest friends and fans.

Most people are always seeking for excuses to go out and meet more friends. And, if you organize trips and dinners, you'll be easily building a great list of followers to your events.

Make sure you're not just a DJ but also a great friend to have around. Being popular as a DJ isn't just about recognition in music, but also personality. You must be a kind, friendly and confident leader above all things. But, you must also know how to control yourself, especially in subjects regarding music and your work. So, avoid drinking in public, and if you do, don't abuse alcohol.

Some musicians may become arrogant with their popularity and abuse it. So, you must be aware of it and avoid getting addicted to the power of having everyone attention on you.

It's important to gain control over the importance others may give you and to keep the reputation you have in reasonable standards.

Choose your friends well and don't allow too many people to get closer in your life before passing the good-friends test. Your best friends will help you keep your head in balance and deal with all the popularity you'll be getting.

Don't be afraid of such fame and allow it to come!

MANAGING SUCCESS

In order to get used to that higher dose of fame and reputation, learn to keep more experienced people around you, as they'll teach you about their own life experiences and what you should prepare yourself with.

Keep also the love you have for music inside you and on top of everything, as a maximum priority in your life, even regarding relationships, because people may abandon you and disappoint you, but the love for music stays forever and can only grow.

The love for music will never let you alone and won't allow you to suffer, no matter what happens in your life, even if you lose all your friends, family, house and money.

"It's a passion, and it goes beyond liking, and beyond a hobby. It's about a way of living... Music is essential" (Armin Van Buuren).

Eminem, the most popular rapper of modern times, has been homeless and starved to pay his debts and food, was abandoned by his girlfriend and family, but during all that time, music was the only thing he had and it kept his heart warm and his mind clear. So, if you can't love music, stop playing it!

It's not worth to waste your entire life for something you don't love. But, if you do, then learn as much as you can about it, so that you can create a path for yourself; a path to success!

There's no path in DJing without success, as the competition is too fierce and the opportunities to scarce.

You must be serious about it and know that developing a career within DJing is something only a few can accomplish.

There are too few jobs for so many talents. There's not other choice but to be the best!

DREAMING WITH A FUTURE

While playing your music at home, in your privacy, dream with your ideal performances, dream about what you want and the future you would like to have!

The music you play should inspire you first, before and above anyone! And, if you remember this, your dreams will change your mind and uplift you!

This is how you prepare yourself to deal with fame and success before it comes to your life. But, also how you program your mind to be inspired with ideas and insights about what to do in your performances!

You must learn to get addicted to the music you love and then control that addiction without getting overdosed and burn in your own uncontrolled fire. If you can do that, you can master a very high energy that music brings to you and feeds you with! It's this mastery of higher energies that creates fame!

I used to be so addicted to music, that I would simply forget to eat, drink or use the toilet, for more than 7 hours. It was like my body didn't exist; it was a very spiritual experience!

Nevertheless, people's attention on you, will bring more energy towards your life, as they focus their own energy and thoughts on you.

So, be a master of that as well, and your inner fire will keep burning powerfully towards a progressively and never ending glory of achievements that will never cease coming to your life, unless you stop them, if you choose to.

That's how you conquer the skill of having a growing popularity and extensive reputation. In other words, feel like the best, act as the best and be the best you can be!

Before being an example to others, be it first to yourself!

You must be your own hero!

Be the DJ you'll like to admire! Be your own vision and become it!

Printed in Great Britain
by Amazon